End!

The Last Judgment

Prophesies come to life!

CONIE TAYLOR

ISBN 979-8-88685-898-3 (paperback)
ISBN 979-8-88685-899-0 (digital)

Christian Faith Publishing
832 Park Avenue
Meadville, PA 16335
www.christianfaithpublishing.com

Printed in the United States of America

To God and His angels for choosing me, a common
person, for being my friend, provider, protector, and
strength, for inspiring me during times when I lost focus,
times when I sought an easy way out rather than facing
those who rejected and ridiculed me in disbelief

*And behold, I come quickly; And My reward is with Me,
to give every man according as his work shall be.*

—Revelation 22:12

CONTENTS

ACKNOWLEDGMENTS

To my dear wife, Loretta, for standing by me and for assisting me in this endeavor. *To Mama Ward* for being there for us both.

THE MISSION

My mission is much like that of John the Baptist, "Another voice crying in the wilderness," for your best interest!

Another forerunner for Christ, only this time, for His Second Coming, the final call for salvation and survival!

INTRODUCTION

God spoke to me in His powerful voice like thunder! From that time until now, He has communed divinely with me by prophetic measures. He even sends His angels to visit me.

This book reflects a true story. I was reared in a small town, Thomaston, Alabama. I went to live in Harvey, Illinois, at age fifteen and started to learn carpentry. Then I came to Detroit at age eighteen and continued in carpentry. I was married at age twenty and started indulging in fast, city life and crime at age twenty-four. This landed me in the federal institution at Sandstone, Minnesota, at age thirty-two.

Sandstone is where it all started. Shortly after I had experienced the power of the Holy Spirit, I had a dream of Christ coming in the clouds!

Since then (during the past fourteen years—from 1996 until 2000), He and His angels have given me a fuller understanding of the past, present, and future up to the final separation of the human race. For instance, the Great Tribulation period faces us soon, of which the false prophet (son of Satan) shall rise into a world power. Chaos!

God is now compelling me to share these things with you in the hope to assist you in salvation, preparation, and survival until Christ returns. This book may be used as a guide to help you make better choices for your future.

PROJECT END TIME SURVIVAL KIT!

*D*estruction is occurring here, near and far, like never before. Is it really getting our attention? Over the past seven years, we've witnessed drastic changes (*disasters*, *lack*, and *inflation*) throughout the world. At this rate, let's imagine what life will be like by the year 2010. Chaos! Much of what was offered just months ago has suddenly vanished! The world conditions are changing at a rate much faster than society is adjusting to. Most are still stuck in yesterday's life, frustratingly losing the battle to the reality of what present life really offers. Society is struggling like never before, mostly because they're simply unprepared to face so many sudden changes.

During these end times, the reality of prophecy is saying that times are not going to get better sufficiently throughout the world, but harder times are on the way until Christ's Second Coming. Until then, this book is designed to assist you in preparation for the worst.

By nature, man has longed to survive and has had good success through time. Tools and strategies used to assist in survival have varied. Working along with the rest, truth, knowledge, and foresight are the most powerful combination offered in this book. After reading this book, you will have obtained more than enough to survive, and if put into good use, you shall dwell among the best survivals.

1. *Will one's belief determine how well he may survive?*

   We believe that one's belief in God the Father, His Son, Jesus, and the Holy Spirit open doors to salvation that this is the first step toward survival. Beginning and establishing a good relationship with God is to our advantage. It is He who will speak to us, guide us, deliver us, and protect and sustain us through each day. All powerful, universal forces know all, see all, and hear all, is definitely an advantage to have as a friend. He can help us entertain the wisest thought and make the wisest decision at any given time, even when we don't realize it. That's what benefits most when we seem powerless and uncertain, yet He directs our footsteps. I wouldn't leave home without Him.

2. *How will being mental and physical fit help us to survive?*

   We believe the mind and body functions are distinct and separate, yet they work as a combination. Both must be fed properly and well-nourished for best results. "You are what you eat" holds much truth. What the mind takes in usually signals the body to carry out the command, positive or negative. What the body takes in has much to do with how good it feels and how good it works. The body needs proper rest and exercise to take on the stress and strain that comes along with each day. To achieve even the smallest goal, mental and physical fitness works to our advantage.

3. *Can sobriety play a big role in survival?*

   A body clear of toxins may move with vigor to take on heavy tasks rather than the feel of defeat and excuse. A mind clear of toxins may render clearer thinking, which amounts to better decision making, not to mention the decision to put money to better use rather than wasting it on drugs, alcohol, cigarettes, etc.

4.   *How effective role can love and unity play in survival?*

We believe that tragedy and hard times have always brought out the purest form of love and unity. Families, friends, and neighbors clinging together in love and unity is an old-fashioned method that has been most effective in terms of achievement and survival. The failing economy, inflation, disasters, sicknesses, diseases, tragedy, and many more will cause more people to humble themselves. You will notice more older children still living at home, more people living in one home, neighbors becoming friendlier, more and people clinging together prayerfully just to make ends meet.

5.   *Will unnecessary spending wreck my survival plans?*

We believe that if you don't need to spend money, you shouldn't because you may need every penny more sooner than you think. Deal with priorities, and if you can get around buying anything that you really can't afford, it's best not to overly burden yourself with unnecessary debt. Start separating assets from liabilities and start cutting liabilities, even if it's a too expensive pet, a car, a credit card, or a longtime friend or family member who borrows money but never pays, who borrows tools but never returns them. The weight that you may have carried with ease will likely weigh up to a ton down the stretch. Those who are quick to wage war may first check to see if they can really afford it. The people and things needed to make survival easier are going to supersede the rest. Cash at hand's reach is going to play a big role. This is to say that it would be very unwise to entrust banks, credit unions, or anyone to hold all your money and assets, in case they go out of business or skip town.

6. *Will owning property work to my advantage?*

We believe that, in most cases, it's better to buy that if everything checks out to be an asset and not a liability. In the long run, buying may turn out to be cheaper than renting, not to mention that certain properties have the potential to render satisfying profit or income. Owning the right property can give a sense of security. It can set forth a foundation that can be built to any height, even to the sky's limit. If God would give the increase, for there must first be an existence.

7. *How can self-employment help me through these crises?*

We believe that while self-employment isn't for everyone, those who hold the vision know that nothing else will work for them. You know who you are. Usually, there's much more to gain than to lose. For example, living from paycheck to paycheck, week to week, and month to month places you in a field of great limitation. The risk is whether or not it will allow broader challenges and growth, whether or not you will be laid off, fired, or the business shuts down. It's a known fact that having a good job or career is much to be appreciated, but the changing times challenge the consistency of what it may be like tomorrow. A small business may struggle, but at least you are still employed as long as it stands. Becoming your own boss is something well worth looking into; who's to say it couldn't be you? Well, you will never know unless you try, and it may not cost a lot, and you may not need to quit your present job (that if you have one) while seeking.

8. *What graphical area projected to ward the highest survival rate?*

We believe that rural areas will be best for living because there, people can produce much of their own necessities. In the case of nuclear warfare, acts of terrorists usually target the larger impact toward the larger crowd.

9. *How can preparation for disasters better our chances for survival?*

We believe that when disasters strike in any form, we need to be better prepared than the people who faced a tsunami, Katrina, Rita, and others. For example, family discussions to avoid panic. Plan to rely upon a system of communication other than telephones and cell phones because they could be knocked out. Store food, water, one gallon per person per day, first aid kit, flashlight, extra batteries, battery-powered radio, generator, trash bags, keep all supplies together, and keep copies of all important documents: birth certificates, mortgage papers, insurance papers, and family pictures, and keep handy cash and coins. Because of the rising gasoline prices, storing gasoline or kerosene would be a great commodity but store a safe distance away from the home.

10. *How can preparation for nuclear attacks better our chances for survival?*

We believe that eventually, the United States will face the element of surprise and sudden destruction of nuclear attacks! It will be to our advantage to prepare for the worst. First, we would need a fallout shelter. Fallout shelters are made of heavy materials, such as brick concrete or stone and any building blocks that block radiation. Fallout shelters help protect against the destruction of the firestorm and scattered bits of radioactive material (called fallout) in the air after a nuclear explosion. This material is carried by the wind up to hundreds of square miles that can cause burns, sickness, or death.

Emergency shelters. An emergency shelter may be found at some schools, churches, public buildings, etc., which provides less protection than permanent shelters but enough to save lives. This type of shelter can be built if better protection is not available, and if fallout will not reach a community for at least several hours.

An emergency shelter should be in a basement or storm cellar if possible. Otherwise, it can be built in an inner room of a building. First, one or more large, sturdy tables are moved to the area where the shelter is to be constructed. Next, various heavy materials are piled on and around the tables as a shield against radiation. An opening is left among the piles of shielding materials to serve as a doorway. Such materials might include books and magazines, bricks, firewood and lumber, metal appliances, paving stones from a patio, and container filled with earth or gravel. The containers could be boxes, strong sacks, or even dresser drawers. After the shelter has been stocked with water and supplies, the doorway should be blocked from the inside with some of the shielding materials.

Home shelters. A family may build its own home fallout shelter, or several families may share in constructing a shelter. A basement makes a good place for a home shelter because the earth around the building helps block radiation. Two walls of a shelter could be provided by a windowless basement comer. Two more walls and ceiling would complete the structure. A fallout shelter may be above ground or partly or completely underground. In most cases, an underground shelter provides the most protection.

A shelter can be built with any heavy construction material. For example, a basement shelter may consist of walls and ceilings made of solid concrete eight inches (twenty centimeters) thick, brick ten inches (twenty-five centimeters) thick, or wood thirty-two inches (eighty-one centimeters) thick. An aboveground outdoor shelter would require walls of solid concrete about twenty inches (fifty centimeters) thick and a ceiling of the same material about eight inches (twenty centimeters) thick. An underground outdoor shelter should be at least eight inches (twenty centimeters) of concrete or fourteen inches (thirty-five centimeters) of earth above it. Any additional thickness improves the protection provided by the shelter.

Any fallout shelter should have at least ten square feet (0.9 square meters) of floor space for each person who uses it. It also should have a drain, an electrical outlet, and adequate ventilation. An underground shelter should have a mechanical blower to provide fresh air. An aboveground shelter or a basement shelter can be ventilated by leaving an open doorway parallel to it. This wall would help keep fallout and radiation from entering the doorway.

A home shelter should be stocked with a two-week supply of food and water. Equipment and supplies for medical, sanitation, and personal hygiene needs must also be provided. A battery-powered radio is necessary to receive information and instructions from civil defense officials. An outside antenna may have to be installed to provide good radio reception in the shelter. Store extra gasoline or kerosene, but keep a safe distance from the home; underground tanks are recommended.

Other important supplies for the shelter include batteries, bedding, clothing, firefighting equipment, flashlights, tools, and eating utensils. If space permits, various items may be provided to make shelter life more pleasant. They include reading and writing materials, toys and games, and nonessential foods.

Living in a shelter need not be difficult if the proper preparations have been made and if reasonable rules of conduct are followed. The daily routine in the shelter must be supervised, and everyone should share in such tasks as preparing food and keeping the shelter clean. Food and water should be rationed carefully, and cleanliness maintained at all times. Someone in the shelter should know how to administer first aid. The fire must be guarded against, and gasoline or other explosive fuels should not be used for cooking or heating. If a mechanical blower ventilates the shelter, it should be operated on a regular schedule.

Every person should stay in the shelter until radio broadcasts announce that radiation in the area has decreased to a safe level. Fallout loses much of its radioactive fairly quickly. In most areas, people would have to remain in the shelter for only two or three days. They could then go outside safely, at least for short periods. Even in areas of heavy fallout, people could probably leave their shelter after a week or two to perform emergency tasks. Such tasks would include obtaining food or medical care (*World Book Encyclopedia*, F Volume 7, pages 20, 21).

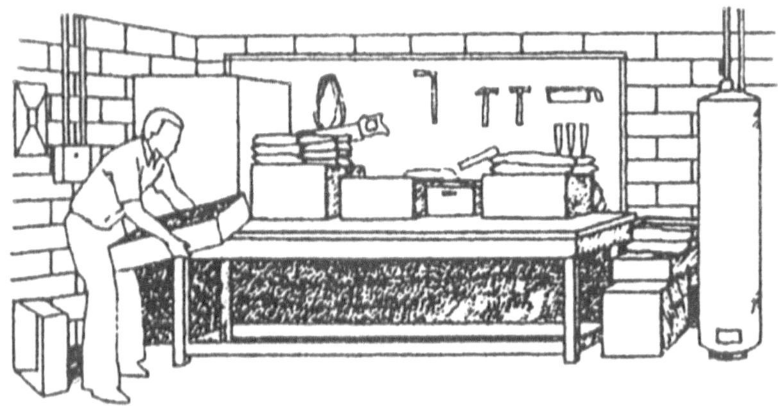

An *emergency shelter* may be prepared by piling heavy materials on and around a sturdy table. Books, bricks, and boxes or dresser drawers filled with earth provide some fallout protection.

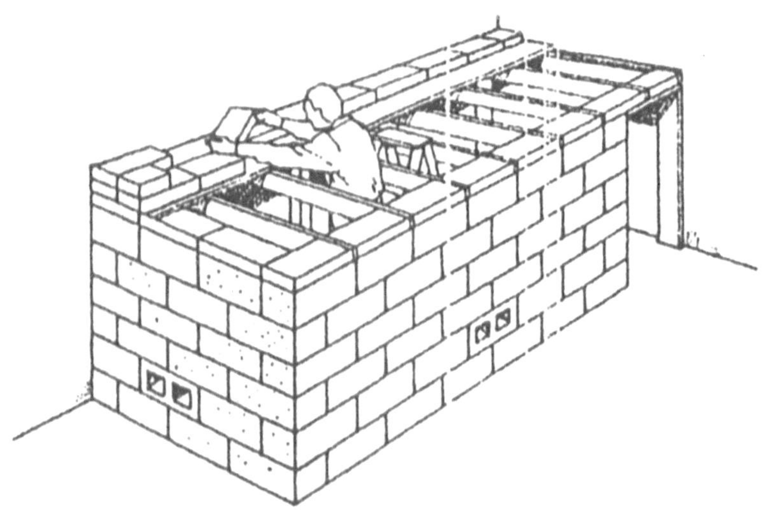

A *basement shelter* may consist of several layers of bricks or of concrete blocks that have been filled with sand. The shelter ceiling should lie below the level of the earth around the basement.

An *underground shelter* may be built with a roof that serves as a patio. The shelter shown above has a trap door entrance at the right of the patio. Some shelters connect with a basement.

An *aboveground shelter* must have thick, windowless walls. The shelter shown above has a shingled roof that covers a thick concrete ceiling. The building also serves as a storage space.

CHAPTER 1

God's Distinguished Voice

The seventh of ten children of Charlie and Sallie Taylor reared in a small town, Thomaston, Alabama. I was born the son of a dirt farmer.

My mother died of a stroke when I was twelve years old, and my father died of a heart attack when I was fifteen years old. With a minimum education, my brother Roy and I moved to Harvey, Illinois, to live with our older brother, Sammie, and his family. Sammie began teaching us carpentry, but after a few years, he moved to Detroit.

When I was eighteen years old and Roy was twenty, we also moved to Detroit and continued in carpentry. Roy and I were doing very well in all aspects of life. A few years had passed, and both of us were married. Roy married a nice young lady named Ola, and I married a nice young lady named Shirley. Their children are Rochelle, Farah, April, and Roy Jr. Our children are Jemone, Shamona, and Tineisha. Roy kept up the good work, but by the time I was twenty-four years old, I had started to experience the fast side of city life. Alcohol, marijuana, and later, stronger drugs, cocaine and heroin, prompted me to commit crimes while trying to keep up the street lifestyle.

By the time I was thirty-two years old, I was indicted by the FBI for altering a vehicle number, which resulted in a prison term of thirty months. I was housed at the federal institution in Sandstone,

Minnesota. A few months prior, at the Wayne County Jail, I had been converted to Christianity.

At Sandstone, during the spring of 1986, I began to conceive a line of divine revelations from God. First, I felt unworthy to receive so much attention from the Creator, Himself. I felt that He should've been communicating with my brothers: Sammie, Henry, Roy, and Lewis. They never did get into trouble. Besides, I had become a master of mischief.

I later understood that God has a purpose in everybody. Apostle Paul, for example, persecuted and murdered the Christians for their belief in Jesus Christ (Acts 8:1–2). Who would've thought that God would've called him to deliver such an important and effective message? God knows all, and He sees things much differently than we humans do. God uses people who are least expected to carry His messages.

In a dream, as some of the old prophets looked, I had intermingled gray and black hair and a beard. Then two snow-white doves appeared before me. I asked the Lord what this meant. "I am calling you to be My prophet, and I am anointing you with double power, to empower you in My ministry. No man shall be able to defeat you or destroy you. I give you power and authority to "Weed out, pull down, destroy, thrown down, build and plant," said the Lord. It was as though I was speaking to God, saying, "Lord, you came sooner than I thought." Amazing! In the blink of my eyes, Jesus was here to redeem His saints.

In a dream, the clouds attracted my attention. They were whiter than any white I had ever seen! Written of the clouds was King of kings—Lords of lords! Immediately, I was in harmony with the godly spirit, having no doubt that this was a message regarding the coming of Christ. But when or what was I to do? This divine contact with His mighty power and the drive to tell what I had experienced was overwhelming. So anxious and excited, I just told it, first, to members of the Christian fellowship, and then to others. "The Lion has roared, who will not fear? The Lord has spoken, who will but prophesy" (Amos 3:8).

In another dream, I had a burning desire to speak as I was pushing my way through a large crowd of people. When I awakened, that same desire was instilled deeply into my soul! From that, I was inspired to write a small message on Christ's Second Coming, copy it, and start passing it out. I worked that until most of the Christians, officials, and inmates were sick and tired of hearing about it. Stafford, a Christian from the Bahamas, would often humor me, asking had the Lord had shown me anything else. He was hoping that I had a revelation about his release from prison.

Then the Lord spoke to me; He actually spoke through me! He awakened me through the night, placing on the tip of my tongue, "Are you waiting on the Lord?" That was an amazing experience too! I was further inspired to search the Bible for its meaning, and I found that it applied to me first, and those who had waited on the Lord had patiently did so by faith. This meant that God had his work cut out if He would equip me with these qualities.

> Surely the Lord will do nothing, but He revealth His Secret unto His servants the prophets. (Amos 3:7)

He spoke to me again, saying, "I will show you all things!" His voice sounded like the roar of millions of people on one accord! So powerful like thunder! Yet He muffled it to my comprehension. Carnally, I pondered, *Oh, how wise this would make me if He shows me all things, only to find out a few years later that He meant understanding regarding His word, His secret things—His work and His Second Coming.* I must admit though that His work zooms in on personal lives, past, present, and future. Some messages are meant to warn that certain events shall inevitably occur, and others are to warn in time to make adjustments. They either bless or curse, build up or bring down. He communicates with me mostly by His word, voice, intuition, dreams, and visions. In some cases, He uses all sorts of people and things to get His messages across. Of course, Satan is always present while trying to distract or deceive me.

In another dream, I saw a huge chicken-featured beast. He walked slowly around me at a distance of about a twenty-foot circle, never blinking an eye. A chilling, goose-bump moment of fear! I immediately felt that this creature represented the dark side. But why had he singled me out to pick on what was bothering me? Well, I was simply glad to wake up in one piece. It haunted me for months. "The creature you saw was Satan. Because you are My anointed, he knows. He has found you to be offensive to his plans during these last days. He has already deceived and destroyed many, and he is set out to devastate the whole human race. He knows that I have called you to warn my people and give them a fuller understanding of My Second Coming," said the Lord.

"But Lord, I'm just a shy and uneducated person with a country accent and slow speech," I groaned.

"Be encouraged, don't be afraid. I, the Lord is with you—the God of Abraham, Isaiah, and Jacob. I shall establish your goings and shall go before you and fight your battles."

"I guess I don't have a choice," I groaned again. "What about all the things I've planned? Drugs, worldly women, stolen property, gambling, etc., don't line up with Your plans. Besides, I love this worldly life, and I'm not really sure I'm ready to quit for good."

But believe it or not—because I didn't at the time—I found myself taking more interest in His godly work. It was like I was under some type of spell. That Bible that my brother Henry had sent to me had become glued to my hands. I had no value for sleep, so inquisitive, and I wanted to find out everything at once. I was hearing echoes of what had been preached about Him in the past—especially from Henry, Roy, and my sisters: Charlie Mae, Bessie, and Mattie. They had struggled overtime while trying to get me to see the light that they had seen. Now my eyes finally had been opened!

After I had learned more about Him and His godly work, I started liking Him, and it was better. The peace I attained from it was a high that I had never experienced before. I was beginning to cherish it as the highest quality of life that, within it, provided completeness. I desired nothing else at the time. Daily, I sought it to escape the pain and misery resulting from prison blues and fleshly indulgence. I had been addicted to many things acting as the higher power over my life, mostly drugs, money, and women. But none of them offered the contentment of that of my newest higher power. I resented the mere thought of it ever slipping from my worldly tight grip because of some mischievous sin or ungodly act.

Called divinely and taught divinely, at first, I thought the people would easily accept me, and this godly work would be easy as eating a piece of cake. But I soon found out that the work of a prophet is much easier said than done. If I'm not fighting Satan personally, I'm fighting his demonic forces in control of people, even in control of some Christians. "That's your duty," God reminds me. So I continue battling the works of evil, thus, fighting a spiritual war that most don't even realize it goes on, breaking curses, pulling down strongholds, and blessing people in all walks of life, thus, making their path easier throughout the world.

"Your notes have accumulated enough for a book, that is what I want you to do, write a book," He spoke softly.

"Me? Write a book? I can't even write a decent letter!" Though I was anxious to try it, not realizing, at the time, that this endeavor would take up to fourteen years.

Prior to my release from prison, I was going through some rough times—feeling lonely and despair because I was without my human fulfillment. During the middle of the night, a Ring of Fire (about twenty-four inches wide upon the wall) awakened me! The flame rotated within the same circle about four feet from me. It was alive! He touched my spirit, assuring me that He was always with me.

Another time, He sent His angel. As I turned over during a restless night, my dreamy, half-awake eyes noticed a small man standing beside my bed dressed in a brown suit and hat. Within that split second of being frightened into a coma, immediately, my spirit identified him as friendly. Still, I couldn't move a single muscle while he remained calm and silent. From a deep sleep, my eyes opened the next morning; that was the very first thing that came to mind. Freshly, I smiled with adoration! It was so obvious that He had brought me peace, comfort, and contentment.

During that time, in a dream, a huge lady stood dormant in the sky. With a golden crown on Her head, She was dressed in pure white. During midday, Her face shined brighter than the sun's rays.

She symbolizes the eternal godhead and the church of Jesus Christ (Revelation 12).

Finally, a long bus ride to freedom, I didn't mind though, just watching the scenery and rejoicing all the way! Through all the turmoil and suffering, I had actually gained from being in prison. God had helped me discover my true character, which is of Christ. His power within enlightened me on how one is completely found in His image while being in harmony with Him. Only then did I see me as the exact same righteous and powerful force in Him. This made me realize that my potential was much higher than I had ever imagined. I had spent a big part of my life following and emulating others, but Christ gave me more confidence in myself.

Would you believe that the same fellow, who I had witnessed Jesus to at first of our journey to prison, was on the bus too? He too had a lot to be thankful for. I recall both his legs being infected from using heroin for eight years. They were swollen as big as two footballs. He had been miraculously healed after I had laid hands on them while praying for him. I had felt such pity and compassion for him, seeing him that way. To witness such a miracle like that, really established my belief even more in my godly friend. He had me sold out, locked, stocked, and barreled. Then He whispered, "What do you think of that, huh? Am I real or what? Look at yourself, haven't I delivered you time after time?"

"Yes, Lord." I remembered every single time.

"Thanks!"

Back home with Shirley, Jemone, Shamona, and Tineisha, we were visited by two angels. One was approximately eight and one-half feet, and the other was approximately six feet, dressed in casual clothing. The larger angel stood quietly in our kitchen and didn't move from that area for the two days as if He was on watch. The smaller angel was very friendly. We sat in the living room, talked, and smiled the whole time as if we had known each other all our lives. He explained everything I needed to know. I understood that God put these two angels and the one before them in my life. They are always with me to comfort, protect, give me messages from God, and help me understand.

On many occasions, angels work through people or pose as people to help fulfill the purposes of God. Apostle Paul reminded us to "Be not forgetful to entertain strangers; for thereby some have entertained angels unawares" (Hebrews 13:1–2). Because of the worsening world's conditions, today, people are so afraid of placing trust in strangers that they sometimes reject God's angelic beings. But believe that during these end times, the very least expected may have to assist you with some food, water, and necessities. They may hold an important message for you. God may desire to bless you through them only. We all shall be put to the test.

And there are times when neither Christ nor my angelic friends seem to be any place nearby. If I didn't know any better, I'd think that there was no God or angelic beings. Suddenly I'm transformed from soaring swiftly like an eagle, back to my weakly human side and back to being a lost chicken who barely flies. Crushed daily by the human race, only my thoughts and visions remain sky-high. They haunt me, seeming to be millions of miles from fulfillment.

"Where are you, my Lord?" my soul cries out! "What sin have I committed this time, oh, Lord? How have I offended you? Why have you hidden your face and blessings from me? My heart is sorrowful, and I've repented quickly over and over! My friends have all turned against me, and even my own family fought against me. Your chosen people hate me for having an understanding of your truth and for standing up for it. The evil and wicked seek to destroy me. There's no place for me to hide. I must face them—even though I'm worn down in distress—with little strength left to fight. My body aches, and my soul is dying! Come to my rescue quickly, oh, Lord, for I'm left to die a slow death in the hands of the enemy!"

Times like this taught me to practice faith in God. I have to base my faith on only His biblical principles and on what He has taught me and has held in my heart. No signs and no intuition, but strictly service by faith. And by whatever means, He always shows up on time. He bows from the heavens and peeps from around the highest mountains, fulfilling all my needs. He breaks the plots of the wicked and removes all barriers set before me. Then He beats them with his strong hands, and as dust against the wind, they fall! Some of them I never see again, and some are brought down to pity and shame. "Oh, Lord, please spare them!" I plead. But who can stop His mighty hands in anger? Who can prevail against the Lord and His anointed?

In a dream, I saw a great earthquake. The earth had opened to a pit of gloom and darkness. Terrified, I shook like a tree's leaf in high wind! I had never imagined what was underneath the very thick layers of earth we walk on every day. About thirty-seven inches of earth, which I stood on, was so stable it didn't move or twitch. Then I looked forward but barely could see the other side of this deep opening. What this was wasn't mystical, but when and where would this occur was what I needed to know. The Lord gave me the understanding that because I stood on US soil, this greatest earthquake shall occur within the boundaries of the United States. Because this event is listed in Matthew 24 as a sign to warn of Christ's Second Coming, sign events shall also occur and recur in many parts of the world when this prophecy is fulfilled.

In a dream, 1989, a huge passenger plane fell about three hundred feet from me. And a helicopter crashed into the ocean. This means that the aircraft shall crash increasingly until Christ returns.

In a dream, a US Government tank had been burned into ruins from battle here in the United States. This means that the United States will be engaged in continuous warfare, eventually reaching US soil, and the impact will be devastating.

And I saw a mighty rushing storm of fire, sweeping away everything in its path. It was so clear and so frightening! We were taking cover in a nearby underground shelter. Boy, was I glad to awake from this dream alive! Relieved, I was to survive such a disaster, especially after so many predicted that only a small number of people could survive something like this. We were prepared though. But what about those who don't believe my report or those who believe and will still be unprepared? "Beware, a great storm is on the way," said the Lord!

In a dream, I saw the closing of supermarkets. In another dream, I saw a cornfield, and some of its stalks were green and fully developed, and I looked further into the field and saw cornstalks, which bared signs of undernourishment. The tall and well-nourished stalks mean a time of plenty of which we now enjoy. The undernourished stalks mean famine and poverty, which will soon affect the whole world. Storms, disasters, inconsistent weather, failing crops, and inefficient production of meats, grains, and necessities will play their part in bringing down the economy. Inflation shall overwhelm society. So believe that wherever poverty increase, there will also be an increase in diseases, plagues, and epidemics of all sort.

I saw the freeways congested to a halt because of chaos and panic! It was all because these people were unprepared. Too many were trying—at the same time—to suddenly escape something awful. Apparently, they had overstayed their survival time in the big cities.

Means of survival may be acted out much more effectively in rural areas—living on farms, learning to raise your own livestock, and producing your own food and necessities. As the poor got poorer and the weak continued to weaken—while living in the big cities—most may not own a ten-foot space to produce anything on. In an effort on mere survival, it would be wise also to plan and build underground shelters, thus storing food and necessities for certain emergencies. Those old-fashioned methods are calling on the human race in their effort to help us be better survivors during these end times. From our present time, we should prepare, for the worst is on the way. Times are coming soon when a side of beef shall become more valuable than all of Queen Elizabeth's wealth.

And I saw, in a dream, a huge stature of a woman floating slowly through the sky. My brother Roy and I were traveling by bicycle. Awestricken we were! The woman symbolizes the image of the beast. The Apostle John also mentioned this same image (stature) and that the false prophet shall rise and bring her to life (Revelation 13:15). When this time comes, he shall dictate and force people to accept his number 666 and worship them. Those who refuse shall be killed (Revelation 13:11–18. See chapter 5, Great Tribulation Stages 1–2). And so believe that because Roy and I were traveling by bicycles, bicycles and motorcycles shall become more popular than ever.

CHAPTER 2

The Fall of Detroit!

*D*uring the year 1989, in a dream, my brother Roy and I saw the fall of Detroit! As we walked on Woodward Avenue from downtown, the buildings looked wretched and abandoned. There were no people occupying the buildings, nor was anyone in sight. The city was barrenly empty and bleak!

Why Detroit? I pondered until God gave me understanding. God's judgment has been upon the city long before now. Detroit is being severely judged for its corrupted and cold-hearted leadership. Its judgment is designed to awake the people for repentance, and its example is meant to forewarn other cities, states, and countries.

Corruptness and coldness of heart are to the bone in this end-time generation, unmerciful, selfish, greedy, and having no compassion or remorse. Although each individual is held accountable for their own acts, God places most blame on society's leaders. He appointed Adam as the first example of leadership and the consequences when leadership fails. We, humans, are still suffering as a result of Adam's defective leadership. The lower vessels suffer most from the end results of corrupted plans on top of plans that originated by defected leadership.

We realize that some of these leaders are not from Detroit and have a powerful influence on how the city is run; for example, the governor and other high officials, even the mob, have a powerful influence over most major cities—continuous, compromising, and bargaining—one favor for another. In this, fairness, mercy, and compassion are usually substituted for greed and selfish purposes, causing the lower vessels to suffer the most.

> David the son of Jesse said, The spirit of Lord spake by me, He that ruleth over men must be just, ruling in the fear of God. (2 Samuel 23:1–3).

This controlling statute uses "must" in command language. "Must," "shall," or "will" is a command word that leaves no space for an exception or human rationale (2 Kings 17:37; Matthew 5:18). Not only does this statute command that we be "just rulers," it also commands that we "fear God" in doing so. "But the Lord your God ye shall fear" (2 Kings 17:39).

This provision was implemented to safeguard mankind from the destruction of wicked, evil, and unmerciful rulers. Thus, it commands rulers to be just and fear God in a respectful manner, observing and trusting in Him as their source of power and a high seat. With the lack of such compliance, they should also fear the consequences which follow that He may dethrone them, if not worse.

However, there are still some God-fearing rulers for the City of Detroit. Some are with the city council and education throughout the city and associates from other cities. For example, I came in contact with some God-fearing members of the city's judicial system: Chief Judge Vera Massey Jones, Judge Dalton A. Robertson, William Cahalan, Bruce Morrow, O'Brian, Crocket, and Hathway, and lawyers: Dawn Ison, John Tragge, Penny Beardslee, Michael Patterson, Jerome Moore, and Jack Van Coevering. I'm sure that there are more God-fearing leaders whose names weren't mentioned. But still, there is not nearly enough to calm God's anger.

Leaders are chosen by God (1 Samuel 16:1) in spite of the political clout or brilliance of men. God blesses from the leadership to the lowest rank of the people (2 Samuel 7; 1 Kings 9:1–8). When leaders deviate from these godly principles—thus falling out of harmony with Him—they tend to lose focus on their real purpose for being in office, "For the best interest of the people" (1 Kings 3:9). Although some lower ranks may show love and concern for the people and the city, they are ineffective if leadership fails. Following are godly consequences (2 Samuel 24:10–16), which cause the low-income, the poor, weak, and innocent to suffer the most. Therefore, for the sake of the people, God has overthrown kingdom after kingdom (see Moses in the book of Exodus).

Detroit, a city that once aided the low-income, the poor, weak, and innocent, has almost given up on them ever becoming resourceful figures in the community. Jesus said, "For ye have the poor (weak and innocent) always with you" (Matthew 26:11). Absolutely nothing should phase out the thought, concern, and support of rehabilitation. When we give up on the ability of God and humanity, we also give up on ourselves. Lower classes of people shouldn't be disdained and demeaned while showing favor to middle and higher classes, predominately whites. One race shouldn't be inferior to another.

Certain classes of people are stereotyped by the vast majority of today's leaders, and their attitude is to get them out of the way through jails, prisons, and many other means at hand. We witness this attitude clearly in government, even tucking away the mentally ill in hardened prisons. But if God would allow this attitude to stand, the overthrow of Hitler was fought in vain. Hitler's attitude is more or less demonstrated through too many of today's leaders, only with a different form of execution. But death is just as essential. This destructive and self-destructive syndrome lacks the rightful solutions. The Bible is simple; however, the first solution is to fear God and look to Him for His wisdom and guidance.

We all fall under the same class, imperfect sinners. And unless we are "justified" by faith through the blood of Jesus, we may never see things in this godly fashion. Only then shall great concern, love, and mercy abound in our hearts for all people alike, regardless of status, race, creed or color.

The City of Detroit, however, has an insufficient flow of legitimate currency to keep the city afloat. Businesses and stores are set up throughout the city and the community, but where are most of the currency flowing? What does it support? You may be surprised to find that most of it flow right out of Detroit to other cities and states, even to other countries. While middle, lower-income, and poor people generally support these businesses, they seldom return proper support to the community that supports them. Usually, it is because most are not residents of Detroit, having little if any real concern for Detroit residents or the city. Many of these businessmen are corrupted to the bone. Racism or some type of prejudice plays a key role in almost every event from one race or another. This most destructive and self-destructive behavior devastates the whole human race.

Mayor Archer seems to believe that casino gambling will be a great asset in creating new jobs and a fresh cash flow in the City of Detroit. This is so true; however, there are significant principles that don't line up, which leads to numerous questions. Will the residents of Detroit be given equal employment? No! Just as usual, when it gets going, you may wonder what happened to equality. Will the cash flow efficiently support the city and its residents? No! Most of the cash will immediately flow far away from Detroit to all parts of the world, supporting just about everything except Detroit, its residents, and communities. Is casino gambling of God? No! In a review of other casinos, it is so apparent that they all breed the pure attributes of Satan. Can the works of Satan revive the fallen city? No! Too much satanic work is why God has overthrown it.

The residents of Detroit will be further cursed with the aftermath of its destruction. An increase in crime of all sorts will call for more jails and prisons. Evil plagues will breed from the roots of casino gambling. Even though casino gambling is legal, the addiction is just as devastating as that of crack cocaine. The strong urge to indulge supersedes priorities and life's values. An average housewife, who has survived the crack syndrome, may now be addicted to casino gambling. She may lose the money she had for bills, pawn her valuables, which she has had for years, and lose her home or car, which may stem domestic violence. Men alike may be beset by this terrible addiction, which is hand in hand with violence and destruction. Leaders who implement this type of remedy for the people, therefore, demonstrate faulty and fruitless leadership.

In the days of King Solomon, he recognized in his heart that the people came first, thus setting forth the standard, "Give therefore thy servant an understanding heart to judge thy people, that I may discern between good and bad" (1 Kings 3:9). Because Solomon's motives were purely in the best interest of the people, God then gave him much wisdom and more wealth. In the contrast, leaders whose motives are driven by selfish love and greed may not seek God's advice and approval in making their decisions. Therefore, Satan guides them.

Too many leaders have almost forgotten another significant principle. Leaders of old times would flock to the prophets and spiritual leaders for prayer and godly advice. If they do so now, it's usually only until they gain a position, then soon forget about the people.

I read that President Clinton and his family appreciate prayer and spiritual guidance from Rev. Jessie Jackson. And I read where President Nelson Mandela—also a God-fearing man—still stands despite all the turmoil he has been through. God-fearing people are usually quick to admit their transgressions and get back in harmony with God, so afraid of the consequences. Just as Kings David and Solomon, for example, were quick to admit sin and repent (2 Samuel 24:10). This is what God expects of today's leaders and of all His people. He's not looking for a perfect human; rather, one who has pure motives and one who's quick to admit sin and repent to Him, thus staying in harmony with Him.

On the contrary, the pharaoh kings were most noted for wicked and ungodly-fearing leadership and the godly consequences that followed. The bottom line is that God has had to constantly destroy wicked leaders just to free His people (see Moses in the book of Exodus). With all these things in mind, we tend to agree that "He that ruleth over men must be just, ruling in the fear of God" (2 Samuel 23:3, supra).

Since the dream about the City of Detroit, God has had me monitor leadership in general, the leaders of Detroit, its community, and residents. Unfortunately, I've found no improvement but continuous decline in demeanor toward the moral standards of God. During the third year of my research, God showed me yet another dream, thus reflecting the end results of its fall. The attitude of the leaders and general population and associates had still declined for the worst. The city was in total ruins as a result of negligence and neglect, with little support and supplies left. Still, they refused to repent to God, having no desire to turn from their wicked ways.

Bear in mind that we are living out a very exclusive time era that was never before during the existence of mankind, the last days of mankind. People are so carried away with their own lives that they give little or no thought to salvation or pleasing God. This is Satan's sole purpose in fulfillment. But because some of God's people are caught in the same web, He must first get attention to separate them in time for salvation and survival. So far, in the past, He has been provoked to anger in doing so, thus, "Rooting out, pulling down, destroying, throwing down, building and planting." Because of the limited time at hand, God is moving much swifter in applying this principle.

For example, weather storms, disasters, and tragedies are hitting harder, even affecting places we least expected. Who would believe that two separate tornadoes would've hit Detroit and Dearborn, Michigan? Get the point! Instead of people asking themselves what is God trying to tell us, they're still running panicky trying to achieve yet more worldly and selfish prosperity. By no means am I suggesting that people shouldn't prosper in worldly aspects or please themselves sometimes, but I'm merely suggesting that God should be first in their lives.

Because Detroit is a fallen city, it shall reward fallen results. There shall be little if any major victories won that would cause great jubilation, lest the people throughout the world forget its fall. Things that would ordinarily flourish shall become hard tasks for many. Many shall prosper, but for most, it's a fall. Many shall deteriorate along with the city, and many shall be led to more promising towns, cities, and states.

Wherefore, after reviewing the necessary facts in this matter, we hold firm to the Biblical principles set forth by God through His prophets, priests, and kings. "He that ruleth over men must be just, ruling the fear of God" (2 Samuel 23:3, supra).

We find the leaders, residents, and associates of Detroit in violation of these principles to the extent of provoking God to anger and wrath. By default—refusal to petition God in full repentance, past, present, and future—this judgment is perpetual; the fall of Detroit is, therefore, affirmed.

Poem-Song

Detroit, the name that once brought stars, putting joy into one's heart before they depart. She has put money in a blind man's can and wealth in a farmer's hand. She had given hope when many had little chance.

Oh, Detroit, you have helped so many! There are some now who have plenty. Some proclaim your name in other towns for personal gain. They say they love—wanting you to act again—like a dove but never really showing you love.

You always give real money and not a token; yet, your heart is always broken. When you give a hundred-dollar bill, they take it and move to the hill. If their wishes weren't fulfilled, truly, they would've been still.

They played ball and lost for a long time without a pause, and we paid dearly to the cause. Finally, they won and began to run as if we all had a gun and took their money to others and had fun!

They think it's smart to avoid Her call, but while She falls, it affects us all! While the city fell, so did the community; this was leaving no opportunity! There will be no one at the city hall to answer your family when they call.

Oh, people, where have you gone?

Remember me? It's Detroit on the phone! The people are leaving because of crime and violence and a decrease in work at the mills. Now, how are we going to pay all these bills? So don't blame me if your wishes aren't fulfilled. Because when I called, everyone stalled, not even thinking that I could fall by the same hands that I fed *all*!

CHAPTER 3

Signs of the End!

*J*esus warned that certain events would occur as signs to warn about the nearing of His Second Coming. Certain events will occur and similarly recur throughout the world. For example, the gospel is being preached. We witness earthquakes, nations against nations, wars and rumor of wars. The hearts of people are waxing colder, and too many people are stressed out and depressed (Matthew 24; Luke 21).

This evidently supports the fact that we're now living out the time of the end and is also proved by today's society. People are reaching out for advice and immediate assistance. They're searching for someone or something to empower their lives or give them temporary reprieve or guide them to victory. If by chance, first choices don't turn out instant satisfaction, most panicky grabs hold of usually the wrong people or things. Too many flock to psychiatrists, psychics, physicians, voodoo, cults, hypnosis, family members, and friends—making them their higher power, rather than the true God. As a result, society is much weaker in godly faith, being more apt to carry out the works of evil.

Their mental capacity and physical ability are failing rapidly because of end time pressures. For example, we witness more incompetence than ever before in the young and the old, seeming as though they're under some type of spell like zombies. The traits of end-time living are mind-blowing and body-shattering. Because of so much lack, Satan is successful in defeating many spiritually, mentally, and physically. I recently witnessed a nineteen-year-old fall flat on his face because of stress and depression. A twenty-seven-year-old fell dead of a heart attack while playing basketball. Their teeth and hair are also falling out as young as age twenty. I could go on and on, but I believe you can identify with my point.

This end-time era is so exclusive from any other time during the reign of mankind because it features the Great Tribulation, the rising of the son (false prophet) of Satan, and the return of the Son of God. So believe that many things shall be happening that ordinarily wouldn't.

Almost everybody is out of control. We now read where the violence rate has shocked the nations and increasing, even in places like Japan, where violence was once considered moderate. Tragedy once thought to be far off is now affecting us in our own homes.

Jesus referred to the demeanor of the people in the days of Noah (Luke 17:26–27) as an example for us to test today's state of violence and evil. As it was in the days of Noah is thus present and overflowing today. Violence and evil have possessed men, women, and children, the young and the old. Seeming like for no apparent reason stems violence in its most hideous form by reason of end-time nature. Not mere coldblooded killers or assaulters of all sort—but they have a "predatory lust" for doing so while finding "pleasure" in it.

Young women are violently killing, hiding, selling, and aborting their babies as though they mean no more to them than throwing away a soda can after enjoying the soda.

This robotically coldhearted generation is on the rise. No morals, no conscience, and no appreciation or respect for human life. No remorse. No repentance. No salvation. No survival. What is the human explanation? They were abused by themselves. What is the biblical explanation? The normal behavior of the end-time generation. Signs of the end!

Children are against parents, and vice versa; husbands are against wives, and vice versa (see Mark 13:12). Strife, violence, and diversity are devastating to many families and people in general. "Every city or house divided against itself shall not stand," said Jesus. As we view the world as our gigantic house and the people as our family, it's very clear that our family is thus divided and deteriorating rapidly.

Jesus also referred to the times of Lot (Luke 17:28-29) as an example to test today's state of iniquity. During the times of Lot, their iniquity—which led to homosexuality, had surfaced considerably boldly. God and Abraham had a discussion about this problem (Genesis 18:20–33).

God later sent two of His angels to the City of Sodom to investigate the people in the hope of not having to destroy them. Lot met the two angels at the front gate of the city and invited them to stay over at his house with him and his family. The townsmen, however, found out about their lodging and made bold attempts to break into Lot's house while trying to rape the two angels of God (Genesis 19). Thus, that put the last nail into their coffin, "For we will destroy this place, because the cry of them is waxen great before the face of the Lord" (Genesis 19:13).

Likewise, Jesus said upon His return that as it was in the days of Noah and Lot, "Even thus shall it be in the day when the Son of man is revealed" (Luke 17:30). He shall destroy all that haven't repented and turned from their evil and wicked ways.

We witness this same persistently bold character in men, women, and children of today's society. Their violent and wicked sins are crying out and annoying God, just as they did in the days of Noah and Lot. Men are marrying men, and women are marrying women. Sex changes are taking place in both males and females. There are many cases of rape among the same sex. Boys are fighting to lay with boys, and girls likewise. If that isn't enough, out of frustration, some lie with both the same or opposite sex. Unnatural. Some men will stand up to Mrs. World Beautiful just to lay with another man, in many cases, more muscular and less attractive than themselves. Likewise, some women overwork their bodies to look muscular and aggressive. Dare real men to speak soft, kind words to them, for they may find them offensive in their frustration!

Homosexuals are now demonstrating and petitioning for gay rights. We agree that they most certainly have a godly right to be loved and treated equally to all humans. Gay rights, however, the

Bible is well settled that homosexuality constitutes sin (Romans 1:18–32). There is no biblical right to commit sin (Hebrews 10:26). In fact, the whole ordeal is biblically, morally, and naturally wrong (Romans 1:25–27).

When I was a child, working in the sizzling hot cotton fields back in Alabama, we'd call homosexuals sissies (unmanly). "My dear (mother), look yonder, eh sissy," we'd say out of confusion. "Com hur boy, hush yo mouth," she'd hollow, minding her own business. We had called the man a sissy because of only a rumor, although he had never acted in a misappropriate manner. Being a sissy in those days was shameful and disgraceful. They felt and acted as though they knew what they were doing was wrong, daring to boldly expose its wickedness to the public. We may fairly say that they feared God, at least a little. But now, you can hardly go any place without being exposed to homosexual acts or advances. The increase in their bold demeanor has migrated through the roof. This was the exact problem in the days of Lot, "The cry of them is waxing great before the face of the Lord."

We realize that rare cases exist where people are proven to have mental and physical birth defects, which is often interpreted to make homosexuality seem normal. But this, itself, doesn't constitute homosexuality. It is constituted when one knows that he's a male or, in case, a female, yet knowingly and willingly indulges in sexual activity with the same sex.

Generations long ago, before our time, indulged in these sinful acts because they rejected God, their loving Creator, "He gave them up to a reprobate (wicked) mind" (Romans 1:24–28), thus cursing humans with the plague of homosexuality from generation to generation (Jeremiah 11:10; Isaiah 14:20–21). This explains how an infant may inherit it, or a young child may develop its tendencies without first being exposed to the act itself. The curse possesses the person first through the spiritual (mind), then controls the body through physical desire and indulgence. Since the Bible describes its activity as being "lustful and selfish," many cases develop from a learned and practiced behavior.

Apostle Paul's views on sexual immorality, he concluded that homosexuals' houses and carries twenty-two other evil spirits:

> Being filled with all unrighteousness, fornication, wickedness, covetousness, malicious; full of envy, murder, debate, deceit, malignity; whispers, Backbitters, haters of God, despiteful, proud, covenant-breakers, without natural affection, implacable, unmerciful: Who knowing they which commit such things are worthy of death, not only do the same, but have pleasure in them that do them. (Romans 1:29–32)

This places homosexuality as the king of lust. However, not only are homosexuals vulnerable to the twenty-two evil spirits listed above but so is anyone else who indulges in any immoral act.

In the reality of today, lust plays a big role in almost everything from the dark side. It may cause one to substitute the true meaning of love and affection, losing life's real value. It may cause a pastor to commit adultery, distract or stop a sermon in its tracks. It may cause a teacher to seduce a student or a student to suddenly murder a teacher. It may cause a father or mother to molest their children or family members to take pleasure in lying with their own kin. The king may cause any of the twenty-two other spirits to take control of the possessed—at any given time—to carry out its evil acts. By all means, have pleasure in doing so; it all depends on just how deeply to the root it has sown its seed.

Good news! However, for those who are possessed by King Lust. There's a provision for salvation, deliverance, and healing through the power of Jesus Christ:

> If we confess our sins, He is faithful and just to forgive us our sins, and to cleanse us from *all* unrighteousness. (1 John 1:9)

> I can do all things through Christ, which Strengtheneth me. (Philippians 4:13)

Just as all sinners and addicts who are possessed by the forces of evil need desperately to be delivered, sex addicts also need deliverance. True deliverance only comes through the *power* of Jesus Christ. The only thing that bothers me now is, do you really want deliverance? A sign of the end is that too many are comfortable in their ways, not desiring to change.

CHAPTER 4

Nature of the Four Horses and Riders

> And he (Angel-Gabriel) said, Go thy way,
> Daniel: for the words are closed up and sealed till
> the time of the end. (Daniel 12:9)

Mystical understanding regarding the end ceased to Prophet Daniel during his time. From that time up to now, God has gradually revealed His secrets to His servants. For example, notice in the following and throughout the remains of this book, the fuller spiritual understanding. This means that the end is very close.

Look at the opening of the first seal!

> And I saw, and behold a *White horse*: and he
> that sat on Him had a *bow*: and a *crown* was given
> unto *him*: and *he* went forth *conquering*, and to
> conquer. (Revelation 6:2)

The *white horse* represents purity, church of Christ—His Holy Spirit and His gospel, its rider (man) represents the Christians, the *bow* represents the power of the Holy Spirit, which the Christians possess, and the *crown* represents the authority that the Christians are given to represent the gospel and triumph over the works of evil; this makes them conquerors through purity and power of the Holy Spirit. When others are conquered by the power of the gospel

(Romans 1:16), they go forth with the same power and authority. Then witnessing to others, thus *conquering* them, and they all go forth to *conquer* (Romans 8:37).

Then the Lamb—Christ, opened the second seal releasing the *red horse* and its rider (verses 3–4). The red horse represents war and bloodshed. Its rider represents people shedding blood, for whatever reason, and people falling as a result.

And He opened the third seal releasing the *black horse* and its rider (verses 5–6). The black horse represents the economy. Its rider represents people in general. The rider is carrying "a pair of balances (scales)," representing the people who keep a close eye on the economy in their fruitless effort to keep a balance. The rider also represents those who fall because of the unbalanced economics.

Finally, He opened the fourth seal releasing the *pale horse* and its rider (verses 7–8). The pale horse represents death and hell. Its rider represents people who are overridden by death and hell.

The representations of these four horses and riders were released by the Lamb—Christ, from seals one through four. There are seven seals in total. The seven seals, overall, represent stages through which the church of Christ traveled from its beginning, featuring Christ, the Christians, the unbelievers, and people in general. At this point, the church has traveled to the latter part of the fifth seal. We can see clearly that the opening of seals six and seven are still future (Revelation 6:1–17).

The riders on the white, red, black, and pale horses, these people, make up the world's population. The spiritual nature of the red, black, and pale horses and riders is in opposition to the whole human race. There's no gain or lack of opposition in regards to salvation and godly prosperity. Surviving constant attacks from either of the spirits of the three horses and their riders may only be done by the will of God.

So the spirit of the red horse and rider overrides the human race with violence, war, and bloodshed.

The spirit of the black horse and rider overrides the human race with unbalanced economics: lack of necessities, famine, hunger, sicknesses, diseases, and epidemics.

And, of course, the spirit of the pale horse and rider has been very persistent in overriding the human race with death and hell—except for the Christians; they face physical death but not hell.

As we approach the end, the red, black, and pale horses are riding even swifter in their most common and ultimate goal, to override one's body to the gloom of death and his soul to the flames of hell!

Meanwhile, the spiritual nature of the white horse and its rider (Christians) shall still go forth with the gospel of Jesus Christ. They shall go forth in power and authority of the Holy Spirit, thus conquering and to conquer!

CHAPTER 5

Great Tribulations Stages 1 to 2

The Great Tribulation period—mentioned by Jesus and prophet Daniel (Daniel 12:1; Matthew 24:21)—should be considered in four stages. For a better understanding, I will list each stage in sequence and chronological order as they rightfully fit into prophecy—along with each biblical major event from this time until the final separation of the believers and unbelievers.

We are now at the outset of stage 1 of the Great Tribulation, encountering a mild recession. Inconsistent weather, storms, disasters, failing crops, falling economics, inflation, famine, diseases, and epidemics increase aircraft failure, continuous warfare, and rapid failure in humans' mental capacity and physical ability. These things and more will play a strong role in progressing the mild recession into a state of severe depression. The scale of economics will gradually tilt into a no-rebounding position. At times certain areas of the economy will deceptively incline while others decline. Overall survey, however, will show a continuous decline.

Stage 2 of the great tribulation will stem mostly from the works of the false prophet, the son of Satan. The Bible warns that this satanic-powered man must surface to play out his role in the script of biblical prophecy (2 Thessalonians 2:1–4; Revelation 13:11–18):

> And the beast which I saw was like unto a
> leopard, and his feet were as the feet of a bear

and his mouth as the mouth of a lion: and the
dragon (Satan) gave him his power, and his seat,
and great authority. (Revelation 13:2)

This reflects the empowerment of the son of Satan. He's now fully grown, living in some part of the world. Although he's a part of the beast, he, himself, is not the actual beast (Revelation 16:13). The beast is their (satanic force) unholy spirit, Satan the father, false prophet the son, beast, their unholy spirit.

Thus, the false prophet's identity has not been revealed. However, he's expected to flatter, con, and manipulate his way to office and power within a short span of time (Daniel 11:21). His forces will start out considerably small to others, so he will be taken for granted (Daniel 11:23). But because he shall exercise all the power of Satan (Revelation 13:1–2), he shall crush his opponents in battle. Elements of surprise!

No one knows just how long it will take before the false prophet rises into full power, but he is expected to be operating sometime in this generation. For one to turn focus on a man holding a specific office could become misleading. However, we can surely be on the watch for a man holding or coming into a high enough position to influence and dictate to people throughout the world. Thus, having a Hitler-like nature.

God chose me to help (sound the alarm) warn the human race to prepare themselves for harder times and prepare to meet this satanic-powered man and prepare to meet Jesus.

Believe also that it's a biblical fact that Christ shall return rapidly thereafter the reign of the false prophet (Daniel 12:7) (Revelation 12:14; 13:5).

The false prophet shall use his satanic powers to make fire fall from the sky (Revelation 13:13). He shall also bring the woman statue to life (13:15), thus deceiving many into believing that he's the Christ. He shall force people to worship the (woman statue—his rules and worships) images setup by the beast and accept his number 666 in their right hand or on their forehead (Revelation 13:15–17).

He shall possess the majority of the human race, influencing and dictating his will throughout the world. I dreamed that Satan, himself, was in the darkest corner of a room filled with people. Only after I pled the blood of Jesus, commanding him to release the people, that parts of his body become visible. His ugly, crustridden hands had long fingers and claws as big as jumbo jets. Only then did he begin to move them away from the people, slowly, like a gigantic drawbridge.

The greatest tribulation upon the believers will result from their refusal to accept his number 666 and his worships. By this, they will be denied the right to "buy, sell, or trade" (Revelation 13:17). Only the believers will have faith enough to reject, and only the believers will be led as lambs to be slaughtered by him and his unbelievers (Revelation 13:15). At that time, there will be only two classes of people considered, believers and unbelievers.

Believers, who will be wealthy, having plenty, will suddenly be forced to leave it all and run into hiding. I dreamed that a basement full of us Christians was hiding in a ragged farmhouse with very little to survive on. Chaos! Husbands, wives, children, family members, and friends will betray each other to face death (Luke 21:16). They will assault and kill close-knitted loved ones in view of each other in their effort to scare people into accepting the mark and worshipping the beast and his images. The slaughter shall be great!

Finally, at the end of his reign, the false prophet and his followers' time shall be up:

> And except those days should be shortened, there should be no flesh saved; but for the elect's sake those days shall be shortened. (Matthew 24:22)

CHAPTER 6

Great Tribulation Stage 3

*I*n stage 3 of the Great Tribulation, the coin turns, but only the unbelievers will suffer and die.

> And when He had opened the seventh seal there was silence in heaven about the space of half an hour.
> And I saw the seven angels which stood before God; and to them were given seven trumpets. (Revelation 8:1–2)

At this time, the seven angels will intervene in the evil works of the false prophet and his followers. Then the 144,000 believers—who will still be alive—will be sealed (Revelation 7:1–4). The seal will be for their protection (Revelation 9:4) because they will still be living on earth during this time.

The sound of trumpets (verses 1–6) each shall introduce a different judgment upon the unbelievers (Revelation 8–9) for accepting the number 666 and for worshipping the false prophet and his images (Revelation 14:9–10). But notice, the judgments of the six trumpets could take months to fulfill (Revelation 9:10). And Christ will not appear in the clouds to redeem His believers until after the sound of the seventh last trumpet. (Revelation 10:7; 1 Corinthians 15:51–52).

Once the unbelievers accept the number 666, thus sets a no-return course for their lives. They then will take on the full nature of their evil and deceptive masters, all condemned. During judgment of the six trumpets, even through most severe pain and agony, they will refuse to repent (Revelation 9:20–21). And they will desire to die, but death will not be permitted (Revelation 9:6) until after the sound of the sixth trumpet (Revelation 9:18).

There are many schools of thought in regards to which will occur first, the Great Tribulation or Christ's Second Coming. The Bible list clearly the Great Tribulation occurs first (Matthew 24:29–30), then Christ's Second Coming (Matthew 24:31). This biblical teaching rules out any chance of the believers escaping the "time of trouble, such as never was since there was a nation even to that same time" (Daniel 12:1). In the very same verse, Prophet Daniel noted, "And (during) at that time *thy people shall be delivered, everyone that name shall be found written in the book of life.*" Apostle John affirmed:

> And He said to me, These are they which
> came out of great tribulation, and have washed
> their robes, and made them white in the blood of
> the Lamb. (Revelation 7:14)

The angel explained to John that the Christians would be rescued at the end of stage 2 of the Great Tribulation. The theory of a pre-rapture (ascending up) occurring before the outset of stage 3 of the Great Tribulation (Revelation 7:14) lacks biblical support. "I beheld, and the same horn (see Revelation 13:11–15) made war with the saints, and prevailed against them" (Daniel 7:21). Be mindful also that Christ shall appear only *once* in the clouds to redeem *all* His believers (Revelation 14:14–15). There is no biblical support for a part two (ascending up) rapture of the believers.

There's a great risk in relying on such presumption that we Christians will just be zapped up without having to face severe adversity from the works of the false prophet. This is Satan's plan to catch people off guard. Master of deception, his traps have longed been set. He will drag his nets as fishermen would at sea.

Sudden destruction!

CHAPTER 7

Christ's Second Coming

Shortly after the seven angels with the seven trumpets—sound trumpet one through six of the judgments upon the unbelievers—the sound of the seventh last trumpet will introduce Christ's Second Coming (Revelation 10:7).

During this event, Christ shall not walk on earth again. Rather, He shall appear in the clouds to everyone (Revelation 14:14), wearing a golden crown on His head. Then He shall send His angels to gather *all* of His believers (Revelation 14:16; Matthew 24:31).

This event is also called the first resurrection; *all* of the dead believers will be raised first (1 Thessalonians 4:16), and the 144,000 live believers will ascend up together to meet Christ in the clouds (Thessalonians 4:17).

I dreamed that a beam of light was slowly drawing us Christians into the heavens! The passage of ray wasn't all over, but it was shaped like a perfectly round circle. This was the only passage to heaven that only God knows this route, Mr. Universe, Himself!

Through this heavenly passage, which all the believers will travel to our Father, Christ, and His angels, will take us to Him. And we shall live there with them for a thousand (millennium) years (Revelation 20:4), thus fulfilling our Father's salvation plan.

During this time, all the souls saved prior to Christ's Second Coming will be released from behind the golden alter that sits before the throne of God (Revelation 6:9–11). They will be matched with their new glorified bodies (1 Corinthians 15:51–52). All the saints of God will be perfectly united for the first time.

CHAPTER 8

Great Tribulation Stage 4

While Christ and His angels deliver the believers safe and sound to the Father in heaven, the seven angels with the seven trumpets will introduce yet more pain and agony upon the unbelievers by means of the seven last plagues (Revelation 16).

So determined to escape the severe punishment, they will think that any place else will ward relief. Their conditions will be at their worst state, but their attitude will remain much the same. They shall blasphemy the holy name of God and still shall not repent (Revelation 16:9–11).

The dragon (Satan), the beast (satanic force), and the false prophet (son of Satan) will plot together in their biggest effort to overthrow the kingdom of God (Revelation 16:13–14). They will gather all the unbelievers on one accord for the battle (*great day of the Lord*) at a place called Armageddon (Revelation 16:16).

CHAPTER 9

The Great Day of the Lord
Joel 2:1–11 and 2 Peter 3:10

*T*hen Christ and His angels will come back out from heaven (Revelation 19:11–16). At His Second Coming, He will be wearing only one crown and will be sitting in the clouds (Revelation 14:14). But at this event, He will be wearing many crowns and will be riding a white horse prepared for the great battle at Armageddon.

As a result, Christ and His angels shall prevail over Satan and his followers. And the beast and the false prophet will be thrown into the eternal lake of fire (Revelation 19:20)!

Then Christ and His angels shall kill the remaining unbelievers (Revelation 19:21). And they will put Satan into prison (hell) for the thousand (millennium) years (Revelation 20:1–2). What a miserable, dark, and gloomy place of fire and brimstone! Yet hell is considered only a holding place for the wicked until they are ultimately thrown into the lake of fire (Revelation 20:15).

Then Christ and His angels shall return to heaven to live with the Christians for a thousand years. Because Christ has promised the Christians that they will spend exactly a thousand years with Him in heaven, the time doesn't start to run until He and His angels return to heaven after the battle at Armageddon. So actually, the Christians will spend a little more than a thousand years in heaven but only a thousand years while in the presence of Christ.

Additional to heavenly praise and worship, the saints will have a duty to perform during their heavenly reign. They will participate in setting final judgment for the fallen angels (1 Corinthians 6:3) and the unbelievers (Daniel 7:22; Revelation 20:4).

Schools of teaching have surfaced regarding the whereabouts and functions of the fallen angels of God. The most popular theory projects them as demonic spirits serving Satan. The Bible states clearly, however, that they have been in hell all along in chains, waiting for their day in court (2 Peter 2:4; Jude 1:6). The satanic force apparently has its own ability to produce its own demonic spirits (Revelation 13:1–2, 14–15, 16:13).

During the thousand years, the earth will be desolate. There will be no life on earth during this time (Isaiah 24:1–3). The Christians will be in heaven (Revelation 20:4). The beast and the false prophet will be in the lake of fire (Revelation 19:20). The unbelievers will all be dead (Revelation 19:21). And Satan will be in prison in hell (Revelation 20:1–2). After "Heaven (the sky) is departed as a scroll" (Revelation 6:14–16) and the "Earth is burned" to sanctification (2 Peter 3:10; Joel 2:1–11), no form of life will be able to survive such devastation! So believe that the earth shall be empty and desolate during the millennium.

CHAPTER 10

Completion of the Millennium

*A*t the completion of the millennium, the Father, His Son, and all their saints will return to earth (Jude 1:14).

Then God shall make a new sky and new earth because He will have destroyed the old ones (Revelation 21:1–5). The New City, Holy Jerusalem, which Jesus has promised, will descend from the sky (Revelation 21:2). This will be the permanent home of the godhead and all His saints forever!

And God will resurrect (bring back alive) all the dead unbelievers (Revelation 20:5). Their souls, which will be held in hell, will apparently be summoned to match their unglorified bodies. This will be the second resurrection, in which only the unbelievers will participate (Revelation 20:6).

Then Satan will be released from hell—prison (Revelation 20:7). What a relief it will be after being tormented for a thousand years. But would you know that he will still have that same old nature? He shall deceive the unbelievers yet again but for the last time (Revelation 20:8).

What nerve they will have by trying to approach the New City in their last attempt to overpower the kingdom of God and His saints (Revelation 20:9)—only to be turned away by extensively hot flames of fire! As a result, the old master of deception will finally be thrown into the lake of fire (Revelation 20:10) to join his son and their beast. Satan was stripped of his unholy spirit at the outset of his thousand-year prison term to hell; therefore, his last attempt will be spiritual powerless. "Blessed and Holy is he that hath part in the first resurrection: on such the second death (resurrection) hath no power" (Revelation 20:6). Only by nature shall Satan and his followers are on one accord at this time.

CHAPTER 11

The Last Judgment

*A*nd Christ shall sit on "The White Throne" and summon the fallen angels and all the unbelievers for trial. He's the true God who implemented the order of law and due process. His procedure is "fundamentally fair." He shall, by no means, "find the facts" of guilt or "judge and commit" without a fair trial (Revelation 20:11).

During this time, the books will be opened—including the book of Life (Revelation 20:12). Initially, from birth, everyone's name is recorded in the book of Life. If during their course in life, they should fail to accept Jesus as their Lord and Savior, their names are blotted out of the book of life (Revelation 3:5).

The Christians will have helped prepare the records of the fallen angels and the unbelievers during their stay in heaven. Every single event that occurs during one's life on earth will be recorded. The main focus, however, will be on the unbelievers whose names will have been blotted out of the book of Life.

One after another, their name will be called to face Him that sits on the throne, "From whose face the earth and the heaven fled away" (Revelation 20:11). This is the one who warned them that His Father had sent Him from heaven to be their Savior (Matthew 18:11), and that salvation was only through belief in Him (Acts 4:12). But they didn't believe. This is the one who warned them that a relationship with God the Father could be established only by acknowledging Him first as God the Son (John 5:23). But they rejected Him, calling Him mere man or just a prophet. This is the one who warned them that His Father had placed all authority and judgment in His hands (John 3:35, 5:22); still, they took this valuable information for granted.

At the trail, just visualize His expounding all these things to the unbelievers, how they have rejected Him and all He represents. During this time, "Every knee shall bow and every tongue shall confess that Jesus Christ is Lord" (Philippians 2:10–11)! Though their confession will come much too late for salvation. Thus, if everyone must ultimately confess to the Lordship of Jesus Christ, it would profit much to do it willingly and timely.

Imagine the death angels being the busiest at the rate of the young and old being called by God to die today. Who knows who will be called upon next? We shall all live forever, but where should be our most concern? An old ironic saying, "All dressed up but no place to go." I'm afraid will turn out to be just irony, having no truth to it. Surely many have been dressed up in their very best attire while waiting for their most precious date, but no show except sudden death! As a result, their eternal living soul instantly awoke to either the heavenly paradise or to the torment of hell fire (Luke 16:19–31)!

To make sure that you are traveling the right road, it would be wise to examine yourself this very moment. A simple test is to ponder. Will Christ require my life this very moment from this earth state? Am I ready to face Him? Your own heart will render an impulsive answer. If you doubt a good chance, you may need salvation. Let us, therefore, honestly apply the following scriptures this very moment to be sure:

> If we (freely) admit that we have sinned and
> confess our sins (to God), He is faithful and just
> to forgive us (all) our sins, and to cleanse us from
> (all) unrighteousness. (1 John 1:9)

> For with the heart a person believes (adheres
> to, trust in, and relies on Christ) and so is justi-
> fied (declared righteous, acceptable to God) and

with the mouth he confesses (declares openly and speaks out freely his faith) and confirms (his) salvation. (Romans 10:10)

For whosoever shall call upon the name of the Lord shall be saved. (Romans 10:13)

You can always trust God to keep His word that you are saved by belief. If you believe you are saved after applying this provision for salvation, then you are indeed.

The final judgment for the unbelievers, however, will be to live forever in the eternal lake of fire! Even death and hell will be thrown into the lake of fire (Revelation 20:13–15). Make the right choice.

CHAPTER 12

The New City and New World

*L*ife in the New City and New World will be eternally different than that of the old. The saints will be like God and see Him as He really is. No more pain, sorrow, crying, birth, or death (Revelation 21:4). No more need for rest or sleep. No more human need or desire. However, family members will still recognize each other (Isaiah 65:23). And the considered most vicious and deadly animals—nowadays—will become harmless and peaceful (verse 25), even the serpent.

The tree of life—which Adam and Eve lost through transgression—shall also be restored along with another. Just as it did in the Garden of Eden, the trees of life will serve as a source of life in the New City (Genesis 3:22). They will bare twelve types of fruit every single month, with their leaves being used for healing the nations (Revelation 22:2).

The crystal-clear water of life shall run as a river from the throne of God amid the golden street (Revelation 22:1). Eternal food and drink for eternal bodies.

No night or day. No sun, moon, stars, or clouds. No electrical power or appliances. God's glory shall light up the New City and New World (Revelation 21:23). The saints shall praise and worship God the Father and God the Son forever!

An amazingly beautiful city! Its glamour and perfection are beyond my fullest imagination! Still, I'm enraptured by what I do understand and by what I can imagine! Its outer appearance is lined with all types of precious stones. It has twelve gates faced with pearls, and its inside walls and streets are made of transparent gold (Revelation 21:19–21).

Jesus proclaims Himself as the bridegroom (Mark 2:19–20). He and His bride personally invite all to attend their wedding supper, which will be held in the New City (Revelation 19:7–9).

> And (Christ) the Spirit and the Bride say, Come, And let him that is athirst, Come, and whosoever will, let him take the Water of Life freely. (Revelation 22:17).

We meditate upon this rich invitation and wish to enter into those gates of the New City to attend their wedding supper. Our carnal thought may easily lead us to prepare for a wedding much like we do today. But our spiritual thought may enlighten us that the bride is the Holy City, New Jerusalem (Revelation 21:2–10), and the bridegroom is Christ. So we should prepare for a Spiritual feast. The wedding supper will simply be one's existence in the spiritual city to thus feast on all that it offers, being glad that you made it there.

The Christians are already considered to be married to Christ (James 5:7), so there's no need for a second marriage. Therefore, when Christ gets hitched at the wedding supper, it will only be symbolic. He, Himself, represents the bride, the bridegroom, and everything that is offered at the wedding supper, including the Holy City.

So believe that the saints will enjoy life in the New City and New World of 1,500 miles range (all directions, including height (Revelation 21:16). For the first time, the meek shall truly inherit the earth. The newly enriched earth (Isaiah 65:21–11) shall ward the saints' much production. We shall fashion our own homes and grow produce and flowers, thus enjoying all of God's creation in its eternity. Imagine life being millions of times better than that of Adam and Eve before the fall, lack of human desires. We shall live a perfect life of love, peace, and harmony, forever!

Behold, I come quickly: Blessed is he that keepth the sayings of the prophecy of this book. (Revelation 22:7)

And, behold, I come quickly; and My reward is with Me, to give every man according as his work shall be. (Revelation 22:12)

Blessed are they that do His commandments, that they may have right to the tree of life, and may enter in through the gates into the City. (Revelation 22:14)

Amen! Amen! Amen!

EPILOGUE

*I*f John F. Kennedy were here, he probably would encourage us to "Ask not what our country can do for us, but ask what we can do for our country."

If Dr. Martin Luther King were here, he probably would direct our attention to his dream of someday colored children and white children holding hands, working together in love and unity.

Today, I'm trying to direct your attention to salvation and survival.